MARRIAGE GOD'S WAY

A Creation Model Approach to Christian Marriage

By Daniel Wynter, B.Th

One Printers Way
Altona, MB R0G 0B0
Canada

www.friesenpress.com

First Edition — 2023

Unless otherwise stated, all Bible quotations within are from the King James Version of the Holy Bible.

ISBN
978-1-03-918484-8 (Hardcover)
978-1-03-918483-1 (Paperback)
978-1-03-918485-5 (eBook)

1. RELIGION, CHRISTIAN LIVING, LOVE & MARRIAGE

Distributed to the trade by The Ingram Book Company

TABLE OF CONTENTS

Dear God,

I pray for those who are reading this book for the first time.

Open their spiritual eyes and ears to the leading of the Holy Spirit as they seek to understand Your will for their lives.

Help them to demonstrate their understanding of Christ's example through their actions and behaviours.

I pray that they will understand the importance of mutual submission and respect in marriage, as outlined in Ephesians 5:21–33.

May they love and honour one another as You have called them to do, and may their marriages reflect Your love and grace.

Guide them through the challenges and joys of married life, and transform their hearts and minds with Your truth.

Fill them with Your love, joy, and peace as they follow You and serve one another.

In Jesus Christ's name I pray,

Amen.

INTRODUCTION

When asked to define marriage and what it represents, most people have a tough time providing a clear, succinct answer. They understand, of course, that marriage is a formal union between two consenting adults—one that unites them legally and financially. They use words like "government sanctioned" and "ceremony" and eagerly describe the importance of "passion" and "commitment" in a contractually agreed upon union.

What these folks don't realize, however, is that marriage is not defined by the state; it is defined by God. Marriage is not a social construct, as secular definitions would have us believe, and it certainly wasn't devised in modern times. It is not merely a civil agreement uniting couples under man's law. Marriage originated with God. As a sacred institution, it binds a man and a woman in a lifelong covenant, both with each other and with God.

Christians understand that when God gifted marriage to humanity, He did so to ease Adam's loneliness and provide him with a suitable helpmate and life partner. He did so to create a nurturing environment in which to procreate and fill the earth with His family. And He did so to present humanity with the gift of earthly companionship.

Yes, God designed marriage for all these reasons, but what many Christians don't know is that He had a far greater purpose in mind. Beyond satisfying our basic human needs and desires, God created marriage to reflect and proclaim the gospel.

Within God's original design for marriage, there is a clear hierarchy and distinct set of patterns He expects us to follow. Unfortunately, over time, these patterns have become altered and distorted to the point that they are almost unrecognizable. Today, there is a profound misunderstanding of these patterns and how they should be demonstrated. Lacking this knowledge, couples live their married lives unaware of God's true expectations for them.

Modern couples often see the creation model approach to marriage as rigid, oppressive toward women, or out of step with contemporary norms. Rather than demonstrating God's patterns as He intended, these couples interpret them their own way or allow Satan to manipulate and misuse God's original blueprint. Even those with the best intentions fail to achieve the ultimate purpose of their marital union, which is oneness with God.

The unfortunate consequence of this lack of spiritual direction is a widespread crisis in Christian marriages. Sadly, people of faith are separating and divorcing at unprecedented rates. Clearly, Christian spouses are not immune to the issues faced by non-Christian couples. Problems such as cheating, communication breakdown, workaholism, financial strain, and lack of work life balance are as pervasive in Christian marriages as they are in secular society.

Marriages today are struggling for many reasons, and so-called experts are falling over themselves trying to understand why. They respond by throwing around terms like "toxic masculinity," "gender inequality," and "women's rights." Somehow, these have become the go-to phrases to explain why marriages fall apart. These factors play a role, of course, but they don't explain why almost 50 percent of North American marriages end in divorce.

I believe that placing the blame on external factors shifts responsibility away from where it really belongs—with Christian couples themselves. It's time for couples to take a hard look at what they're doing, or not doing, and to repair and strengthen their marriage on a spiritual level. Rather than letting the secular world define what their marriage should look like, it's time to remodel marriage based on the blueprint laid out in God's original design.

As a pastor and faith-based marriage counsellor, I regularly work with couples experiencing marital troubles. During weekly counselling sessions,

I am witness to the different kinds of challenges they face. Regrettably, husbands and wives often blame each other or stubbornly refuse to see their partner's perspective. I hear countless stories of a wife's lack of intimacy, for example, or a husband's failure to be a loving and supportive spouse.

In most cases, neither spouse has taken time to evaluate their own thoughts and behaviours and how they may be contributing to the situation. Instead, they sabotage their relationship and get stuck in an endless cycle of resentment and blame.

During these weekly sessions, I offer guidance, hope, and encouragement to clients as we work through their marital struggles. Because I see life through the lens of Scripture, I integrate Christian philosophy into every therapy session. I am guided by the knowledge that it's only through the wisdom and strength of the Holy Spirit that couples will begin to heal their relationship. I am driven to inspire them to apply God's laws and patterns correctly so that they can move toward spiritual wholeness and oneness with our Lord and Saviour.

While it's a blessing to be able to sit with clients in a face-to-face setting, I recognize that not everyone has the means or opportunity to benefit from in-person counselling. Some people are too busy, while others find face-to-face therapy difficult. In writing this book, I want to provide an additional resource for couples feeling disconnected or frustrated in their marriage. What's more, I want to offer realistic, practical steps to help them strengthen their relationship with each other and deepen their connection with God.

This book demonstrates that reclaiming God's original design for marriage is the *only* way to heal your relationship and achieve your spiritual purpose. In the coming chapters, I'll explain how God's design for marriage became distorted through history and why learning to embrace His original model will set your marriage back on the path to spiritual healing.

Together, we'll examine God's original marriage principles, as found in Scripture. These are the same principles my wife and I have successfully applied to our marriage for many years. Following His principles correctly has brought us closer to God and protected our marriage from unholy influences. By correctly applying them in your life, you too will gain the knowledge and tools to experience the light of God in your marriage.

Through an analysis of Scripture, I will methodically lay out the patterns contained in God's original design. I'll explain the significance of His biblical principles and how couples can apply them to both honour God and enhance their married life. These principles remain as relevant today as they were in biblical times. Following them correctly will lead couples to a marriage built on love for each other and a commitment to Christ. Whether you've been together for decades or are just starting a life together, the first step in protecting your marriage is reclaiming God's original design and learning to walk with Him in your daily life.

For men struggling to understand their purpose in marriage, I offer practical steps to reclaiming their role as head of the household and spiritual leader in the home. For women buckling under the weight of impossible demands on their time, I provide concrete solutions to restoring peace and balance in their lives. For couples wanting to draw closer to their Creator, I offer spiritual guidance and a pathway to greater intimacy with God.

Finally, this book demonstrates the importance of following God's instructions exactly as He instructed. Through verse analysis, I will clarify what obedience means and why God views it as the ultimate expression of our love for Him. Using biblical examples, I'll demonstrate that God greatly rewards those who obey His instructions and swiftly punishes those who defy His commands. We are all subject to God's laws and patterns, and we must adhere to them as much in our marriage relationships as we do in our everyday lives.

Folks, marriage is hard, and marriage is complicated. Anyone who believes otherwise is being unrealistic and will surely be let down at some point in their lives. We are all lost souls, navigating the rocky terrain of our relationships. However, I firmly believe that if you love God, if you learn to obey His patterns as He instructed, and if you are both committed to the covenant you made with Him, there is nothing you can't achieve as a married couple.

It is my hope that this book will serve as the North Star through this process, a spiritual compass, guiding you closer to God and helping your marriage to stay on course. I hope and pray that you use the tools I provide here to embrace God's purpose for your marriage and place Him at the centre of your union. Fulfilling God's intended pattern for marriage will unlock your potential as a couple and establish the foundation of a blessed and happy union.

CHAPTER 1

The Rise of a Worldly View of Marriage

"Therefore shall a man leave his father and his mother, and shall cleave unto his wife: and they shall be one flesh." (Genesis 2:24 KJV).

The Bible paints a clear, indisputable picture of God's original design for marriage. In fact, Scripture tells us that marriage is an essential part of God's plan, a divine institution that provides couples with mutual joy, partnership, and security.

Marriage, as such, is a beautiful gift from God, presented for the purpose of partnership, procreation, and the raising of children. "Therefore shall a man leave his father and his mother, and shall cleave unto his wife: and they shall be one flesh." (Genesis 2:24 KJV).

But for Christian couples, marriage is about more than a practical commitment between two people. It is symbolic of the deep and loving relationship between Christ and the Church. In fact, God intended husbands and wives to directly model their marriages after the relationship between Christ and His Church: "*Husbands, love your wives, even as Christ also loved the church, and gave himself up for it..*" (Ephesians 5:25 KJV).

MARRIAGE IN BIBLICAL TIMES

In biblical times, modelling a marriage in this way was easy to do. Husbands and wives had distinct roles, which were biblically ordained and well-defined, within the marriage. Husbands were responsible for providing their family with food, clothing, and security: *"But if any provide not for his own, and specially for those of his own house, he hath denied the faith, and is worse than an infidel."* (1 Timothy 5:8 KJV). Wives were expected to submit to their husband's spiritual leadership, manage household duties, and love and nurture their children. *"She openeth her mouth with wisdom; And in her tongue is the law of kindness."* (Proverbs 31:26 KJV).

For thousands of years, this division of duties was closely observed, which contributed to the strength and stability of marriages. Men supported their families with physical and financial security. Women provided maternal support and fulfilled their domestic responsibilities within the home. As old-fashioned and chauvinist as this may sound today, the man's role as breadwinner and the woman's role as nurturer were the accepted societal norms of the time.

LOVE MATCHES IN THE VICTORIAN ERA

These functional roles remained unchanged until the late seventeenth and early eighteenth centuries, when the concept of marrying for romantic love emerged and eventually became more fashionable than marrying for religious interests or family lineage.

Encouraged by the philosophical ideas of the so-called Age of Enlightenment, people began to marry to satisfy their own personal desires, rather than to serve God. That is, marriage went from being a sacred institution to a secular contract. During this period, marriage became less about pleasing God and more about pleasing the two people involved in the relationship.

This idea of marriage primarily for the sake of romance and emotional satisfaction reached its height during the Industrial Revolution. Interestingly, this emphasis on "love matches" and "personal happiness above all" corresponded with a steady rise in the rate of divorce.

By the Victorian era of the mid-nineteenth century, people no longer saw marriage for religious purposes as the social ideal. By this time, not only was romantic love viewed as the primary reason for marriage, but a cultural construct that could be changed and redefined with the times. These ideas heavily influenced and shaped the modern marriage patterns we see today.

THE SOCIAL AND ECONOMIC IMPACT OF TWO WORLD WARS

It was during the twentieth century, however, that the institution of marriage took a dramatic new turn—one that was based on a new wage economy. The economic pressures of World War I forced men to leave their jobs to help with the war effort and women to move into the workforce to fill the empty positions they left behind.

The sheer scope and magnitude of the war was unlike anything experienced before, and the endless warfare had horrific consequences for families. Millions of men were killed or became invalids on the battlefield. Women were forced to step out into the world, to adapt, and to learn new skills for the survival of their families and countries.

To support their families and keep the economy moving, women went to work in traditionally male-dominated industries, including manufacturing and agriculture. Overseas, they contributed to the war effort by working as nurses, doctors, translators, and ambulance drivers.

Even though women were demonstrating their ability to perform "men's work" outside the home, their wartime efforts were considered a temporary solution to the labour shortage of the wartime crisis. After World War I, most women returned to their domestic roles to make way for the returning men. As it turned out, however, War World I was a turning point for women, who could not ignore the social and economic opportunities they had gained as a result of the war.

The war mobilization during World War II had a similar impact on women's roles in the workforce and their desire to contribute financially to their families and the economy. During the Second World War, women were once again called upon to enter the workforce in mass numbers to fill jobs left empty by men who were fighting in the conflict.

Once again, there were opportunities for women to enter a broader range of occupations— the types of jobs that had never been open to them in the past. They were not just working in traditionally female dominated jobs (teachers, domestic workers, secretaries) but in jobs that kept society moving (bank tellers, streetcar drivers, construction workers) and in highly specialized male-dominated fields such as medicine, law, and engineering.

By the end of World War II, it was clear that women were not returning to their traditional roles as expected but were in the workforce to stay. Despite the discrimination they faced, women continued to fight for equal pay for equal work, for the right to higher education, for opportunities to work in non-traditional fields, and for full equality under the law. In the postwar era, their roles in the labour market continued to expand, and today, women make up almost half of the global workforce.

MARRIAGE IN THE POSTWAR ERA

The huge shift in the economic structure resulting from two world wars transformed the roles of husbands and wives. In addition to increased job opportunities, the feminist movement of the 1970s, expanding equal opportunity laws, and greater access to education all served to solidify women's quest for equality and independence.

As women's roles in marriage were changing, the expectations for men were changing too. As women began to take on the role of breadwinner, men were left feeling directionless and confused about their own responsibilities within a marriage.

No longer were men considered the sole or primary financial providers for their families. At the same time, the women in their lives were no longer content to be homemakers and caretakers; they were out in the world making their own money, contributing to their family's financial well-being and, in some cases, making more money than men.

Men's masculinity, which for centuries had been tied to their ability to perform as breadwinners, was now being called into question. Where it had been expected for men to "put on the pants, go out into the world, and bring home the paycheque," now many women were contributing to their family financially.

As a result of these changes, the functional roles of husbands and wives became blurred and distorted. Today, men are under enormous pressure to find new ways to define themselves within the confines of their marriage, while women are struggling to meet their responsibilities both at home and within a workforce that includes greater prospects for promotion and financial gain.

IN PRAISE OF THE BIBLICAL CONCEPT OF MARRIAGE

As we've seen in this chapter, marriage today is quite different from marriage in biblical times and throughout much of human history. Where once it was seen as a precious gift from God that symbolized the relationship between Christ and the Church, now it is considered a cultural construct that can easily be updated and redefined to suit the social impulses of the day.

Where once it was viewed as a pathway to serving and glorifying God, now it is seen as a way to satisfy individual romantic desires above all else. Personal happiness has become the main goal of marriage and, at the same time, the role of men and women within marriage has become distorted and blurred.

As women's role in the workforce changed due to the economic pressures of two world wars, so did their role within the institution of marriage. No longer restricted to the domestic sphere, women moved out into the workforce, gaining a new level of independence and economic security that did not depend on having a husband.

Likewise, men's functional role with marriage was transformed. No longer were they the key providers of women's financial security. Rather than acting as spiritual leaders, as God intended, many men became toxic and abusive in their provider role, expecting that because they were the bread-winners, they were entitled to exert complete dominance over their wives and control every aspect of her life. These men completely lost sight of what it means to be spiritual head under God's original design.

What is men's purpose in a modern marriage? What functional role should they play in their relationships? How do we reclaim God's original design in a world where women are levelling the playing field and men are struggling to find their footing and design?

While women's push for workplace equality was necessary and commendable, there's no denying that the blurring of marital roles brought about instability and uncertainty in modern Christian marriages. As the accepted societal norms of men as breadwinners and women as homemakers collapsed, men no longer knew how to be husbands, and wives no longer wished to be tied down to their traditional role within the home.

The result of all this turmoil and confusion is on clear display when you look at the current state of Christian marriages. Today, we see fewer young people choosing to get married, fewer children being born into stable Christian families, and higher divorce rates than at any other time in history. This is what happens when you allow the world to define what a marriage should look like instead of upholding God's original standard.

Despite the social and economic changes that we've discussed in this chapter, adhering to God's original standard remains the only way to achieve a strong spiritual union. But what, exactly, is this standard? What does the Bible say about God's original plan? Think about your own marriage. Are you closely following these principles, or have you been influenced by the modern marriage patterns that are common in secular culture?

The following chapter explores the fundamental principles of God's original design for marriage. Beginning with the first marriage, God put forth a template for His divine institution that would set the standard for all future marriages. We'll examine the significance of family and children within this template and look closely at God's order of authority and the importance of adhering to it within a godly marriage.

We'll learn that in God's original design, marriage was viewed as a permanent, unbreakable union. We'll examine why this is, and why Christian couples today need to recommit themselves to this ideal.

Finally, we'll see that God's original design not only served as a template for Christian marriages, but a prediction of the bond between Christ and the Church. Understanding this principle will help us recognize the importance of emulating Christ in our lives and marriages.

By learning the key components of God's marriage patterns, we see the value of rejecting a worldly view of marriage and reclaiming God's original design. In the coming chapters, you'll see how to do this and how to apply His original principles to build a stronger foundation for your marriage. By taking the focus off yourself and placing it on God, you'll be equipped to address any challenges within your marriage. By fostering a God-centred marriage based on His original standards, you'll build a healthy, lasting relationship that serves God's purpose.

FREQUENTLY ASKED QUESTIONS

What does the Bible say about God's original design for marriage?

The Bible tells us that God's original design for marriage is as a sacred institution and a precious gift that provides mutual joy, partnership, and security. It is also a divine institution that serves as a model for the deep and loving relationship between Christ and His Church.

Why is marriage considered an essential part of God's plan?

Marriage is essential to God's plan because it serves as a symbol of the bond between Christ and the Church. It also provides couples with mutual joy, partnership, and security while fulfilling God's intended purposes of partnership, procreation, and raising children.

What is the purpose of marriage?

According to Genesis 2:24, marriage provides companionship, mutual support, and the creation of a new family unit. Therefore shall a man leave his father and his mother, and shall cleave unto his wife: and they shall be one flesh.

How should Christian couples model their marriages?

Christian couples should model their marriages after the relationship between Christ and His Church. According to Ephesians 5:21-End.

What were the traditional roles of husbands and wives in biblical times?

In biblical times, husbands were responsible for providing their family with food, clothing, and security, while wives were expected to submit to their husband's spiritual leadership, manage household duties, and nurture children.

How did the concept of marrying for romantic love emerge and affect the institution of marriage?

The concept of marrying for romantic love emerged in the late seventeenth and early eighteenth centuries, eventually becoming more fashionable than marrying for religious interests or family lineage. This trend led to marriage becoming less about pleasing God and more about satisfying individual desires.

What were the social and economic impacts of World War I and II on the roles of men and women in marriage?

World War I and II had significant social and economic impacts on the roles of men and women in marriage. Women had to enter the workforce in mass numbers to fill jobs that had been left empty by men who were fighting in the war. This contributed to women gaining a new level of independence and economic security that did not depend on having a husband.

How did women's roles in the workforce change during the twentieth century?

Women's roles in the workforce continued to expand during the twentieth century, and today women make up almost half of the global workforce. This has contributed to the blurring of traditional marital roles.

What is the current state of Christian marriages?

The current state of Christian marriages is unstable, with fewer young people choosing to get married, fewer children being born into stable Christian families, and higher divorce rates than at any other time in history.

How can Christian couples build healthy and lasting marriages based on God's original standards?

To build a healthy and lasting marriage based on God's original standards, Christian couples should reject a worldly view of marriage and embrace His original design. They should adhere to God's order of authority, view marriage as a permanent, unbreakable union, and model their relationship after the bond between Christ and His Church. Couples should also prioritize putting God at the centre of their marriage and work together to foster a God-centred relationship.

CHAPTER 2

Reclaiming God's Original Design

"For this cause shall a man leave his father and his mother, and shall be joined unto his wife: and they two shall be one flesh" (Ephesians 5:31 KJV).

Couples today face endless decisions when it comes to marriage. Without a road map to follow, many are left feeling bewildered and alone. Without a template to apply, their questions often go unanswered. How do I know if I'm ready for marriage? How do I approach parenting as a God-fearing Christian? What does it mean to sacrifice for my wife or submit to my husband? How does God view divorce, and what will it take to make my marriage last?

I believe that the answers to these questions can be found within the biblical principles of marriage. Only by learning and applying these principles will we gain the wisdom and tools to make the right decisions about our married lives.

As we've seen, marriage is not a man-made construct. It did not emerge from nothingness to satisfy people's romantic desires. It was not meant to be easily modified or amended by the winds of time. Marriage was devised by God to serve His purpose and, therefore, cannot be separated from its original design. What's more, God's original design contains fundamental guiding principles that must be followed to serve His purpose.

But why did God create marriage in the first place? What purpose does His divine institution serve? What are the core patterns and principles contained within His design, and how can we learn to apply them to better serve Him and to enhance our married lives?

Scripture reveals a great deal about the intentions behind God's precious gift and how He intends us to use it. By studying His original design, as laid out in the Bible, we get a detailed picture of God's marital pattern and the benefits of adhering to them as He commanded, even in these modern times.

In this chapter, we'll examine His Word to better understand the fundamental principles contained in the marriage covenant. To shed light on the core intentions behind God's gift, we'll go back to the wedding of the first couple—Adam and Eve. We'll look at how the first marriage came to be, what it demonstrates, and why it should forever serve as the universal template for Christian marriages.

Next, we'll consider how these patterns and principles can instruct behaviour in modern-day Christian marriages. You'll learn to evaluate your current behaviour and determine how to improve it to better to serve God's purpose.

You'll learn how to decide when you're ready for marriage and, if called upon to have children, the importance of teaching them to follow God. You'll learn the meaning of headship and submission within a family as well as the significance of following God's order of authority. For those of you who are contemplating separation from your spouse, you'll gain insight into God's view of divorce and why you should do everything in your power to make your marriage work.

Finally, we'll examine how the institution of marriage foreshadowed the future relationship between God's son, Jesus Christ, and the Church. Scripture reveals that, by design, God intended marriage to form a picture of Christ and the Church. Because this is such a critical component of a

God-fearing marriage, I will lay out exactly what you must do to model the Christ-Church relationship in your marriage.

THE FIRST MARRIAGE: A DIVINE TEMPLATE FOR ALL FUTURE MARRIAGES

The first and most important principle of God's design is that marriage belongs to God. While humanity gets to enjoy its earthly benefits, God created marriage to serve His own purpose. As Christians, we know that God is the Creator of all things. From the book of Genesis, we learn that He created the heavens and the earth. He created the sun and the moon to divide the light from the darkness. He separated the waters from the land and gave life to every living thing on land, in the air, and in the sea.

All of creation was God's design: *"In His hand are the deep places of the earth: The strength of the hills is His also. The sea is His, and He made it; And his hands formed the dry land"* (Psalm 95:4–5 KJV). And all of creation had a purpose. This wondrous, majestic universe that we see before us was formed by God's command, for His glory, and for the enjoyment of His greatest creation—mankind. Once God had built the perfect environment, He looked around and was satisfied and pronounced it "good." This magnificent world He created was now ready to serve as home to His most beloved creation.

It was then that God said, "*Let us make man in our image, after our likeness: and let them have dominion over the fish of the sea, and over the fowl of the air, and over the cattle, and over all the earth, and over every creeping thing that creepeth upon the earth.*" (Genesis 1:26 KJV). And so, God created the first man, called Adam, from the dust of the earth, breathing life into him and giving him complete authority over His creation.

From Genesis, we learn that God is a purposeful God who created the universe for His glory and the pleasure of humanity. But we also learn He is a loving God—a God who understands, profoundly, the needs of mankind. Because God cared so deeply for Adam, He knew instinctively that Adam was lonely. In Genesis 2:18 (KJV), God says: *"It is not good that the man should be alone; I will make him an help meet for him."* God recognized that Adam needed a helpmate and life partner and so created a companion for him, the first woman, called Eve.

To do this, God placed Adam into a deep sleep and opened his side. From his side, He took a rib. This rib was used to form Eve, who was to serve as Adam's companion and helper. So, God created Eve, not from dust as He had with Adam, but from part of Adam's body. Indeed, Adam's response when God brought her to him was: *"This is now the bone of my bones, and flesh of my flesh: she shall be called Woman, because she was taken out of man"* (Genesis 2:23 KJV).

The first woman, then, was created for Adam as a lovely gift from God. And Adam must have loved her deeply! This wonderful being was presented to him, formed from his own body and designed to be his perfect companion. Adam recognized immediately that theirs was a profound union and, as such, their bond was instant and deep. This intimate union—the first marriage—was ordained by God and would serve as a template for all future marriages.

Ready Yourself for the Gift of Marriage

A second principle of God's design for marriage is that people must prepare themselves spiritually before entering into the covenant of marriage. An important part of a man's preparation involves finding his vocation or life's purpose. In fact, a man is not prepared for marriage until he is in his God calling.

This was as true of the first husband as it is of husbands today. Through Scripture, we know that before God brought Eve to Adam, He took certain steps to ensure Adam was prepared to receive his bride. By the time God presented Eve to Adam, He had already provided Adam with clear direction and purpose for his life.

Adam's first job was caretaker of the Garden of Eden: *"The Lord God took the man and put him into the garden of Eden to dress it and to keep it."* (Genesis 2:15 KJV). God also entrusted Adam with the immense responsibility of managing His creation. This included giving Adam the task of naming God's animals: *"And whatsoever Adam called every living creature, that was the name thereof. And Adam gave names to all cattle, and to the fowl of the air, and to every beast of the field"* (Genesis: 2:19–20 KJV).

Adam's vocation, his God-given purpose, was overseeing the Garden of Eden and caring for God's creation. By cultivating and taking care of the garden and, later, by observing and classifying God's animals, Adam was proving himself a worthy servant and an excellent steward of God's creation. Notice that only after Adam understood and began to fulfill his God-given role did God determine Adam was ready for a helpmate.

Men today must look at marriage in the same way. Rather than jump headfirst into a lifelong commitment, a man should first ready himself for marriage. And again, in the eyes of God, a man is not prepared for marriage until he has found God's calling for his life.

Unfortunately, many men marry without a vocation or sense of direction for their lives. And when their wife, who is designed to be their helpmate, suggests options, these men become frustrated. *Why does she keeps suggesting things,* they wonder, *and why is she trying to control my life?* Well, she's recommending things because you haven't given her anything to help you with! You have no direction. You've not grounded yourself with any sense of purpose. And as your helpmate, your wife is hard-wired to help you better yourself.

In fact, it was for this very reason that Eve ate the forbidden fruit from the tree. She ate the fruit, not because she was wicked, but because her very nature was to better Adam. When the serpent promised she would gain all knowledge and become more like God, she was enticed because she genuinely believed her actions would help her husband in the end.

Before a woman is ready for marriage, she too must ready herself. To do this, she must build herself up spiritually and make herself presentable. What does this mean for the modern Christian woman who wants to be ready for marriage? In essence, it means that before she marries, she must become independent so that she can be a true helpmate to her husband.

Remember, before God presented Eve, she was just a rib, one part of a whole. By the time she was presented to Adam, however, God had built her up to be a powerful companion to her husband, assisting him in caring for all creation, and ready to bear and nurture his children.

Regrettably, women today often present to men as spiritually incomplete. They are that metaphorical rib, broken and unfinished. As a Christian woman preparing for your future marriage, focus on your spiritual wholeness. Pursue Christ and learn to walk with Him in your daily life. Learn to stand on your own two feet in every aspect of your life.

Don't surrender to the antiquated teaching that insists you require a man for salvation and fulfillment, becoming a dependent in your relationship. Instead, do the work it takes to become a reliable and effective partner to your mate. Presenting yourself as spiritually whole is one of the best things you can do to help your future marriage succeed.

God's model says that before marriage, both men and women must do the work of self-discovery to prepare for their future spouse. It is only after a man finds his God calling that He will reveal his future wife to him. Likewise, it is only after a woman makes herself spiritually presentable that God will lead her to her husband. And if the spiritual work is done correctly, neither will have to go in search of a spouse. God knows best, and when He feels you are prepared for marriage, He will always demonstrate His will.

Demonstrate Christlike Behaviour for Your Children

We've seen that God's divine template contains all the patterns and principles He considers healthy and acceptable in a Christian marriage. A third principle of this template is that God wants married couples to form their own family unit and expand it where possible.

When God said, "*Therefore shall a man leave his father and his mother and shall cleave unto his wife: and they shall be one flesh*" (Genesis 2:24 KJV), He was stating that, once married, a couple must start their own family and separate from their parents. Within this new unit, the man would serve as spiritual head, and the woman would have authority over her home.

God also intended this new unit to be the perfect space for raising children. After creating Adam and Eve, for example, God blessed them and told them: *"Be fruitful and multiply, and replenish the earth, and subdue it"* (Genesis 1:28 KJV). Having and raising children was not only God's will, but a fundamental reason for marriage. As with marriage, God made the family with His purpose in mind—to celebrate His glory and spread the gospel throughout creation.

Children were not an afterthought but a critical part of God's plan. He saw them as a blessing bestowed upon humanity: ""*Lo, children are an heritage of the LORD: And the fruit of the womb is his reward. As arrows are in the hand of a mighty man; So are children of the youth. Happy is the man that hath his quiver full of them: They shall not be ashamed, but they shall speak with the enemies in the gate.*" (Psalm 127:3-5 KJV). But God doesn't just want parents to have children, He also cares deeply about how those children are nurtured and raised.

More than just conceiving and bearing children, God expects couples to teach their children to become spiritual beings. While having children is not absolute (not everyone is meant to have them), those who do must raise their children to love God and obey His teachings in all things. *"Train up a child in the way he should go: and when he is old, he will not depart from it"* (Proverbs 22:6 KJV). In other words, if you are called to it, having children within the marriage covenant and raising them to be good Christians is a wonderful way to glorify God.

As a Christian parent, it's important to remember that children are spiritually innocent, and it is up to you to guide them toward a relationship with Christ. In fact, your most important job as a parent is to model godliness, so they too will learn to model Christ in their lives.

The Word of God says that the children will be considered holy and clean under the umbrella of a godly parent: *"For the unbelieving husband is sanctified by the wife, and the unbelieving wife is sanctified by the husband:*

else were your children unclean; but now are they holy" (1 Corinthians 7:14 KJV). That is, while your children have not yet come to faith on their own, God sees them as holy precisely because you and/or your spouse have dedicated your lives to Christ.

Remember, a child is not renewed in spirit until they're old enough to understand and accept the salvation that comes from God through Christ. Because their dominant nature is sinful, they innately gravitate toward sinful things. That's why the foundation must be set in the home from the beginning. For children, this foundation is set, not just by hearing the Word of God, but by seeing it demonstrated through Mom and Dad. Watching their parents interact in marriage is their strongest demonstration of the relationship between Christ and the Church.

Children learn spiritual truths related to marriage by seeing how their parents treat one another as they follow God's patterns. While some of this will be picked up in Sunday school lessons in God's house, most of it is absorbed by watching their parents interact in their own home. Yes, all couples have disagreements, but constantly fighting in front of children will have troubling, long-term impacts on their lives. Resist the temptation to lose your temper with your spouse. Instead, find healthy ways to resolve your disagreements. Engaging in positive, loving interactions with each other will give your kids a fighting chance to become holy and sanctified, based on the example you set in your home.

Respect and Follow God's Order of Authority

A fourth principle of God's design is that husbands and wives are intended to have distinct roles within a marriage. These roles were purposely designed to be different, but equal, and to balance and complement one another. Husbands and wives were meant work in unison to achieve one common purpose—the pursuit and glorification of God.

In fact, Scripture is clear about the organizational structure within God's design. In First Corinthians, for example, Paul the apostle speaks directly about God's principles of headship and authority when he says, ""*But I would have you know, that the head of every man is Christ; and the head of the woman is the man; and the head of Christ is God.*" (1 Corinthians 11:3 KJV).

According to this principle, husbands are the spiritual heads of the household. As spiritual leaders, they are expected to demonstrate Christ's love for the Church within their families. Their role is to celebrate God's character by caring for others, providing for their wives, and always putting their family's needs above their own.

It is important to understand that when the apostle refers to the husband as the "head of his wife," he is not talking about the husband exerting dominance over her. Instead, he is speaking of the husband's ability to love and support his wife and his willingness to help her adhere to a way of life that glorifies God.

A wife, for her part, is expected to cherish and support her husband and submit to his spiritual leadership. Throughout Scripture, we see Eve referred to as Adam's "helpmate," a role that carries a great deal of importance and weight. Just as Eve did in biblical times, today's Christian wife must strive to assist her husband in achieving his God-given purpose. As Eve was positioned in biblical times, so is the modern Christian wife uniquely situated to help her husband become the spiritual leader God intended him to be.

Protect Your Marriage to Prevent Divorce

A fifth principle of God's design is that God intended marriage to be a lifelong commitment. As the cornerstone of the family unit, when a marriage fails, the whole family fails. Children suffer and all of society is impacted. While divorce did occur in biblical times, Scripture tells us that God did not approve of it.

In the Book of Matthew, when the Pharisees question Jesus about divorce, Jesus tells them that when a man and woman marry, *"they are no more twain, but one flesh. What therefore God hath joined together, let not man put asunder."* (Matthew 19:6 KJV). When pressed on the matter, Jesus explains, *Whosoever shall put away his wife, saving for the cause of fornication, causeth her to commit adultery: and whosoever shall marry her that is divorced commiteth adultery.*" (Matthew 5:32 KJV). This underscores God's negative view of divorce. In general, divorce is a sin, and the dissolution of wedding vows should be avoided at all costs.

Unfortunately, today's couples often see divorce as a quick and easy solution to their marriage problems. Rather than taking steps to divorce-proof or repair a troubled marriage, they choose to terminate it and move on. God-fearing couples must realize, however, that in the eyes of God, marriage is a permanent, unbreakable union. In fact, God's original standard of marriage as a lifelong covenant remains just as relevant today as it was in biblical times.

While it's true that God makes exceptions for adultery and abandonment, the Bible is clear that divorce must always be a last resort. Christian couples should do everything they can to work through their marital conflicts and remain together. A husband must maintain a lasting, unbreakable bond with his wife just as Christ maintains an unbreakable union with the Church. That is, he must remain faithful to his wife in the same way that Christ remains faithful to His Bride, the Church. It is this mindset that Christian couples must adopt as they strive to repair and heal their broken marriages.

Model the Christ-Church Relationship in Your Marriage

As a companion and wife, Eve became an integral part of Adam's life and purpose. We learned in Genesis that when Adam first saw Eve, he understood immediately that she had been formed from his body and that they were now one entity. "*Bone of my bones and flesh of my flesh*!" he exclaimed as he laid eyes upon her. With these words, Adam revealed that he grasped the significance of God's gift to him.

Adam's remarks here were important, not because they showed that he understood the manner of Eve's creation, but because it was clear that he recognized the sacred and holy nature of their union. Adam clearly understood that their marriage held tremendous significance to God. He understood the spiritual importance of God's divine institution. Not only was this union to become the universal template for all marriages, but it would also foreshadow the coming of God's son and eventual unity of Christ and Church.

A sixth principle of God's design, then, is that human marriage is symbolic of the relationship God ordained between Christ and the Church. In fact, God designed earthly marriage to be the most important demonstration of Christ's relationship with the Church. Throughout Scripture, we see the Church referred to as the Bride of Christ, with Christ as the head of the Church, His Bride. Above all things, for God, the sacredness of marriage was wed to the sacredness of the Church. This is the Christ-Church model couples are expected to follow.

What does this Christ-Church model mean for today's Christian couple? It means that husbands and wives must always look to Christ as the perfect model of how to behave in their marriage. While this process differs for men and women, as God has given them distinctive roles, both are expected to mirror Christ's love of the Church within their marriage.

As the spiritual leader in his home, a husband has the primary responsibility to ensure his marriage demonstrates the Christ-Church model. God intentionally placed men in this position of responsibility, and it is their divine duty to apply the Christ-Church model in their marriage. But what does this entail? How do Christian husbands ensure they are modelling Christ in accordance with God's plan?

In the next chapter, we'll take a closer look at men's functional roles within a marriage. If you are a man who is unsure of your purpose, I'll use Scripture to detail God's expectations for you. For those of you feeling alienated in your relationship, I'll provide steps to establishing a stronger marital relationship. As a Christian husband, understanding your God-given role is key to growing in Christ and demonstrating true spiritual leadership in your home.

FREQUENTLY ASKED QUESTIONS

What is the first principle of God's design for marriage?

As demonstrated by the story of Adam and Eve, the first principle of God's design for marriage is that marriage belongs to God. He created it to serve His own purpose. The story of Adam and Eve, the first couple, demonstrates this principle, as their union was ordained by God and serves as a template for all future marriages.

According to the second principle, what steps should be taken by men and women to prepare themselves for marriage?

According to the second principle, men should find their vocation or life's purpose, which is their God-given calling, before entering marriage. Women, on the other hand, should build themselves up spiritually and become independent, focusing on their spiritual wholeness, and walk with Christ in their daily lives in order to be a true helpmate to their husbands.

What is the significance of following God's order of authority in a Christian marriage?

Following God's order of authority in a Christian marriage is significant because it helps maintain a harmonious relationship between spouses with each person playing their respective role as per God's design. It also ensures that the marriage models the Christ-Church relationship, which is a critical component of a God-fearing marriage, as it aligns with God's intended purpose for the institution of marriage.

What is the third principle of God's divine template for Christian marriages?

The third principle of God's divine template for Christian marriages is that God wants married couples to form their own family unit and expand that unit where possible.

What is God's intention for the family unit in terms of raising children?

God intends the family unit to be the perfect space for raising children, to celebrate His glory, and to spread the gospel throughout creation.

What is the responsibility of parents in raising their children?

According to Proverbs 22:6, the responsibility of parents in raising their children is to train them up in the way they should go; when they are old, they will not depart from it.

What is the significance of 1 Corinthians 7:14 in terms of children and their parents' faith?

1 Corinthians 7:14 signifies that children are considered holy and clean under the umbrella of godly parents, even before they come to faith on their own.

What is the fourth principle of God's design for Christian marriages concerning the roles of husbands and wives?

The fourth principle of God's design is that husbands and wives are intended to have distinct but equal roles within a marriage, balancing and complementing one another as they work in unison to pursue and glorify God.

What is the fifth principle of God's design for Christian marriages with respect to divorce?

The fifth principle of God's design is that God intends marriage to be a lifelong commitment, and divorce should be avoided at all costs, as it is generally considered a sin.

What is the sixth principle of God's design for Christian marriages?

The sixth principle of God's design is that human marriage is symbolic of the relationship God ordained between Christ and the Church, with the Christ-Church model being the one couples are expected to follow.

CHAPTER 3

The Role of the Christian Husband

"Husbands, love your wives, even as Christ loved the church and gave himself for it; that he might sanctify and cleanse it with the washing of water by the word" (Ephesians 5:25–26 KJV).

In chapter one, we observed how society's expectations for men and women have transformed over time. Where once men were relied on as sole providers for their household, today that breadwinner role is shared with—or even taken over by—women. We saw, too, that the large-scale entry of women into the workforce resulted in both positive and negative consequences for families. For husbands, as biblically ordained heads of household, the effects of these changes were particularly destabilizing.

From a young age, men are socialized to evaluate their worth on their ability to act as financial providers. When a man fails to live up to these expectations, not only does he feel judged by those around him, but his self-esteem and self-worth are negatively impacted. When a man's wife takes over the role as breadwinner, he is often left feeling worthless and inadequate. Some men respond with hostility or resentment. Some become depressed or start to question their masculinity, while others start to distance themselves from their wives altogether.

All of this can have serious implications on the health and stability of the family. But what can be done about it? How can we help men regain their purpose and begin to thrive within their marriage? Obviously, women returning to their domestic roles is not a realistic or appropriate solution. If a woman chooses to work and strives to excel in her chosen career, she has every right to do so. The path to healing Christian marriages does not involve relegating women to the home. Instead, we must look toward a deeper understanding of God's true expectations for men and educate husbands to deliver on them correctly.

I believe that to help men become the heads of household and spiritual leaders God intended them to be, we must first take a step back. We must begin by recognizing that false, modern interpretations of God's original design for marriage have caused men to lose sight of their true role. In this chapter, we clarify, through Scripture, God's true standards for husbands so that they can correctly apply them in their lives. For men, regaining their place as head of household goes hand in hand with reclaiming God's original marriage design.

God intended husbands to lead by Christ's example and to model their position of leadership after Christ's position as head of the Church. In fact, there are several principles outlining exactly how husbands should model Christ in this capacity. As a Christian husband, understanding these principles can enhance your marriage and help you reconnect with your spouse on a level you never thought possible.

Once I discovered these principles and shared them with my wife, it transformed the way we interacted with one other. We began to live a life of intentionality, taking every opportunity to demonstrate Christ in our marriage and everyday lives. In doing so, we were ministering Christ and the gospel to those around us. Without saying a word, we were demonstrating how to surrender a marriage to God and model the interaction of Christ and the Church.

PRACTICAL TIPS FOR MEN

In the following sections, I'll provide concrete measures you can take to achieve the same results. These practical steps may seem insignificant or trivial at first, but matching the pattern of Christ and Church will let you harness the potential in your marriage and revitalize your relationship with your spouse. Here are a few specific actions you can take to unlock your best marriage and become a better spiritual leader in your home.

Guide Your Family in the Light of God's Ways

As mentioned previously, a key purpose of the family is to provide a space to nurture children. As one of God's greatest masterpieces, however, the family serves an even greater purpose—to spread the gospel and advance God's Word. Just as with marriage, the ultimate purpose of the family is to exalt God and fulfill His purpose. Every member of a family is called upon to do this, but as head of the household, a husband bears a particular responsibility to guide his family members to live a life that reflects God's greatness.

In chapter two, we learned that God has a clear structure for marriage that places husbands at the head of the household. When the Apostle Paul spoke of God's order of authority, he referred to the husband as head of the wife and Christ as the head of the Church. And when God placed husbands in a position of headship and authority, He had clear expectations for *how* they should lead.

As head of your household, you are to lead your family members—not by dominating or intimidating them—but by emulating the way that Christ interacts with the Church. You are to be a role model in your household, the foundation upon which everything else will stand. This foundation must be based on humility, honesty, kindness, integrity, and respect. Most importantly, as a godly man, you must lead your family in personal worship. Pray with your family, read the Bible together, and do everything in your power to lead them closer to God.

Love Your Wife and Present Her Blameless

In Ephesians 5:25–26 (KJV), Paul reminds men of their divine responsibility to their wives when he says, *"Husbands, love your wives, even as Christ loved the church and gave himself for it; that he might sanctify and cleanse it with the washing of water by the word."* Paul is speaking here of emotional love, of a devotion, humility, and kindness as deep and lasting as Christ's love for the Church. Loving your wife in this way doesn't just allow you to sustain a satisfying and healthy marriage, it allows you to mimic how Christ relates to the Church.

Love for your wife can be expressed in many forms. Regardless of how you choose to show it though, it's important to remember that, besides God, she is the most important person in your life. Treat her as such. Honour and respect her. Appreciate and embrace all the unique qualities that drew you to her in the first place. Spend quality time together where you can share your deepest thoughts and open your heart. This verbal intimacy and private time will create a deep trust and strengthen your bond. Speak softly to her. Even when she makes mistakes, be humble, gentle, and caring. Remember, *"Charity suffereth long, and is kind; charity envieth not; charity vaunteth not itself, is not puffed up, doth not behave itself unseemly, seeketh not her own, is not easily provoked, thinketh no evil;"* (1 Corinthians 13:4–5 KJV).

If loving your wife is the first part of your responsibility, presenting her blameless is the second. This means that, as a godly man, you never speak unkindly of your wife or belittle her in front of others. As Christ was expected to *"...present it to himself a glorious church, not having spot, or wrinkle, or any such thing; but that it should be holy and without blemish."* (Ephesians 5:27 KJV), so a husband is expected to present his wife to others in the best possible light.

When was the last time Jesus exposed the failings of His followers by writing their faults in the sky? Husbands must follow this example. Complaining about your wife, exposing her faults, or badmouthing her is a direct violation of God's spiritual pattern. Instead, you must love her unconditionally, praise her in front of others, and always encourage her to walk with God.

Provide for Her in Any Way You Can

We know that women are perfectly capable of supporting themselves. They do not need to rely on men to put food on the table or pay the bills. In some cases, that responsibility is shared with their husband. In others, it is shouldered alone. We know that the Bible tells us that, as husbands, we must fulfill our role as provider. But if women are financially independent and self-sufficient, where does that leave us? How do husbands serve as providers when our wives are accomplishing so much on their own?

Regardless of whether your wife decides to go out to work or works from home, you can still be a physical provider for her as Christ is a provider to His Bride, the Church. By understanding spiritual patterns, you will see there are many ways to provide for her that are not tied to income or wealth. For example, she may be the one to buy food for the family, but you can provide dinner at the end of a long, exhausting day. She may be the one to pay the rent each month, but you can provide security for the house. Working diligently to share the burdens of daily living (laundry, shopping, raising children, etc.) is a huge step to becoming the committed provider God intended you to be.

Nowhere in Scripture does it specify that the way we provide for our wives must be financial. Look closely at your marriage to see where you can support your wife in ways that have nothing to do with money. Provide a comfortable environment in which she can flourish, the emotional support she needs to grow and thrive, the physical security she needs to feel safe and protected, and a strong shoulder and willing ear to help her take on the pressures of daily life.

Remember, as a godly husband, it is your divine responsibility to love and support your wife and to provide for her however you can.

Demonstrate Spiritual Leadership in Your Home

God gave men the responsibility of being spiritual leaders in their homes. Unfortunately, many husbands are confused about what spiritual leadership really means. To understand this principle, we must first recognize that a Christian husband is entrusted to lead his wife with the Word of God. It is his duty to motivate and inspire her to grow in her relationship with God. He must build up and protect this relationship and guard against the many factors that might tear it down. This is an immense responsibility that far too few men take seriously.

For example, one of the biggest complaints I hear from wives is that their husband refuses to take the lead in prayer. He has become too distracted, they say, preoccupied by the business of living, to pay attention to her spiritual needs. Are you one of these men? Do you sit around watching TV in the evenings instead of taking time to encourage your wife's spiritual growth? Now is the time to change that, and one of the most powerful adjustments you can make to become a better spiritual leader is to lead your wife in prayer.

Begin by understanding the awesome power of prayer. Scripture says, *Pray without ceasing*" (1 Thessalonians 5:17 KJV) because prayer is a fundamental way to mimic the pattern of Christ in the Church. You can begin today! Call a prayer meeting. Lay your hands on your wife and bless her. Read the Word and help her to understand it. If you have children, be available to worship together as a family. Make prayer a regular part of your daily routine. Remember that praying with your wife every day is the simplest, most impactful way to cultivate a relationship with God and demonstrate true spiritual leadership in your home.

Be Faithful in All Things and Forsake All Others

In Proverbs 5:15, Solomon speaks to the importance of monogamy in marriage, advising his sons to be faithful to their wives, regardless of any temptation they may face. Be happy with your own wife, he tells them, "..*Rejoice with the wife of thy youth. Let her be as the loving hind and pleasant roe; Let her breasts satisfy thee at all times; And be thou revished always with her love.*" (Proverbs 5:18–19 KJV). Solomon is arguing here for the value of self-control, for avoiding temptation and the charms of seduction, and for not getting caught in a trap of your own sin. "*For the ways of man are before the eyes of the Lord,"* he cautions, *"And He pondereth all his goings."* (Proverbs 5:21 KJV). *In other words, wherever you go, He is watching.*

We know that God intends husbands and wives to be bound together in a lifelong covenant. He does not look kindly upon divorce and expects couples to be faithful. As a Christian husband, it is incumbent upon you to be committed to your wife as Christ is committed to the Church. Just as Christ is faithful to His Bride by renouncing all other religions, so must you be faithful to your own wife and give your love to her alone. Just as the Church belongs to Christ and is of His body, so must a husband realize his headship belongs to her body alone. That is, he belongs to, and is fitted for, his wife only.

While part of being faithful means never committing adultery, for Christian husbands, faithfulness goes beyond physical monogamy. Being faithful to your wife also means showing reliability and integrity of character. She must know she can depend on you and trust in your words, always. She must see your dedication to her, in all ways, every day. In addition to your fidelity, demonstrating your faithfulness to her in these ways, shows a steadfast commitment to emulating Christ's loyalty to the Church.

God has a purpose for all of us. As a Christian husband, He has called upon you to lead your family. Following the principles outlined in this chapter will go a long way in helping you to fulfill your calling. What's more, you can begin to implement these principles immediately. Love your wife. Protect and provide for her. Consult with her. Devote yourself to her and her alone. Be patient with her. Pray with her. Minister to her and gently guide her closer to the Lord. Build her up, always. Never tear her down. She is your greatest earthly companion and should always be treated as such.

And in all of this, remember, God has given her a purpose of her own. How familiar are you with that purpose? How well do you understand God's expectations for your wife? As you step up to take on the mantle of responsibility God has placed upon you, educate yourself on your wife's role in His marriage plan. Taking the time and making a genuine effort to understand her responsibilities—and the trials she may face in fulfilling them—will only serve to make you a better leader.

In the following chapter, we'll look closely at the role of the wife, according to Scripture. We'll learn about the principles a woman must follow to become a godly wife. For husbands seeking insight into their wife's experiences, the chapter will provide a window into the biblical principles she must adhere to. Most importantly, if you are a woman and a Christian wife in particular, it will provide valuable instruction on how to nurture a God-centred relationship that will help your marriage flourish.

FREQUENTLY ASKED QUESTIONS

How have society's expectations for men and women changed over time, and what are the consequences of these changes on families?

Society's expectations have shifted from men being the sole providers for their households to women sharing the breadwinner role or even taking it over. This large-scale entry of women into the workforce has had both positive and negative consequences for families. For husbands, these changes can be destabilizing because they feel judged and inadequate, which can lead them to feel hostile, resentful, depressed, or can cause them to distance themselves from their wives.

What are some negative effects of men feeling inadequate as providers?

Negative effects can include hostility, resentment, depression, impact on physical health, low self-esteem, potential substance abuse, questioning their masculinity, and distancing themselves from their wives, which can impact the health and stability of the family.

How can men regain their purpose and thrive within their marriage without reverting to traditional gender roles?

Men can regain their purpose by understanding God's true expectations for them as husbands and spiritual leaders. This involves recognizing false interpretations of God's design for marriage and correctly applying God's standards in their lives.

How can understanding the principles of how husbands should model Christ in their marriages enhance their relationships?

Understanding these principles can help husbands reconnect with their spouses on a deeper level, leading to more intentional, loving, and supportive relationships that demonstrate Christ in their everyday lives.

What are some specific actions husbands can take to become better spiritual leaders in their homes?

Husbands can guide their families in the light of God's ways, love and present their wives blameless, provide for their wives in various ways, demonstrate spiritual leadership in their homes, and be faithful in all things, and forsake all others.

How can husbands provide for their wives in ways that are not tied to income or wealth?

Husbands can provide emotional support, a comfortable environment, physical security, and help with daily responsibilities, like chores and childcare.

What does it mean to be a spiritual leader in the home?

Being a spiritual leader means leading the family with the Word of God, motivating and inspiring them to grow in their relationship with God, and protecting and nurturing that relationship.

What are some ways husbands can demonstrate faithfulness to their wives?

Husbands can demonstrate faithfulness by remaining committed to their wives in both physical monogamy and showing reliability and integrity of character, being dedicated, trustworthy, and loyal in all aspects of their relationship.

What is the role of a Christian husband according to Scripture?

A Christian husband's role is to lead his family by modelling Christ, loving and presenting his wife blameless, providing for her, demonstrating spiritual leadership, and being faithful in all things.

How can understanding their wife's role and responsibilities within God's marriage plan make husbands better leaders?

Understanding their wife's roles and responsibilities allows husbands to better empathize with their experiences, appreciate their efforts, and provide appropriate support and guidance, which can lead to stronger and more fulfilling relationships.

CHAPTER 4

The Role of the Christian Wife

"Who can find a virtuous woman? For her price is far above rubies. The heart of her husband doth safely trust in her, So that he shall have no need of spoil. She will do him good and not evil All the days of her life" (Proverbs 31:10–12 KJV).

Women today carry a lot on their shoulders. Increasingly, their push for economic freedom has become a double-edged sword. While there are obvious benefits to economic freedom, becoming more self-sufficient hasn't necessarily brought them more fulfillment and joy. Even in dual-income families, where financial pressures are shared with their husband, women often find themselves doing the lion's share of work. In most families, duties such as childcare, caring for aging parents, and housework still overwhelmingly fall on the wife.

In addition to dealing with workplace stress, women carry the mental load of keeping things running smoothly at home. On top of a busy workday, they are usually responsible for homemaking, caretaking, and making sure everyone in the family is cared for. Doctors' appointments, children's homework, laundry, dishes, kid's sporting and social activities—the list is endless. This double burden (balancing outside employment with domestic duties) can have a negative impact on women's physical and mental well-being.

Women are left feeling stressed and overwhelmed by their endless obligations as workers, mothers, and wives. Without enough support from their husbands, they feel unappreciated, lonely, and trapped in a never-ending cycle of worry. Working mothers carry an additional burden of guilt for not spending enough quality time with their children. And looming over all of this is their belief that there's no relief in sight for their burnout and stress.

It's important to understand that the chaos and confusion women are experiencing is not due to their hard-won economic independence. As with men, it stems from a fundamental misunderstanding of God's true expectations for them within the marriage covenant. What God expects of wives has been distorted by modern interpretations. Like men, women have lost sight of how to honour and fulfill their God-given duties within their marriage.

Are you a Christian wife who is walking this road right now? Do you struggle with communication in your marriage? Do you resent your husband for not supporting you as he should? Are you buckling under the weight of competing demands for your time? Do you feel guilt every time you head to work, leaving your kids in the hands of someone else?

Understand that you are not alone in this. Wives today face unprecedented pressure to "have it all together." Where traditionally, they could focus on serving in the home as wives and mothers, today they spread their time and energy in a million, chaotic directions. But how do we restore order to the chaos? How do we reverse the turmoil women are experiencing and restore a sense of balance and purpose in their lives?

The answer, I believe, lies in helping women understand God's *true* expectations for them with His original marriage design. I'm not talking about the expectations society places on them or even the unrealistic demands they place on themselves. I'm referring to the qualities that God expects them to demonstrate to live a righteous and fulfilling life.

Helping women understand these expectations also means arming them with the knowledge and tools to fulfill their divinely ordained role. Only through Scripture can we uncover God's intended design for women. Remember, the road to a balanced life does not require women to leave their jobs and professions. The road to a balanced life can only be found in God's Word.

PRACTICAL TIPS FOR WOMEN

The Bible lays out several characteristics of a godly woman. In this chapter, we'll examine these qualities in detail so that you can begin to apply them in your own life. Knowing your true purpose and refocusing your attention on God will help fortify and protect your marriage. Most importantly, following His patterns will help you become the true woman of God that He expects you to be. Let's explore some of these qualities now.

Be a Crown to Your Husband: Choose Virtue and Discretion

The last chapter of the Book of Proverbs serves as a guide for Christian women who wish to align themselves with God's Word. In Proverbs 31, for example, as King Lemuel's mother is advising him on how to become a good king, she also describes the qualities he should look for in a wife. A virtuous wife, she explains, is a God-fearing woman who maintains a deep connection to God throughout her life. She is generous and kind, and she always looks to the Lord for advice and comfort. Above all, she is completely devoted to her husband.

Her loyalty to her husband does not allow her to speak critically of him. Rather, she chooses to always remain discreet. Because she wants what is best for her husband, she seeks every opportunity to raise him up in front of others. This makes her an invaluable partner to her husband. *"Who can find a virtuous woman?"* Lemuel's mother asks her son, *"For her price is far above rubies. The heart of her husband doth safely trust in her, So that he shall have no need of spoil."* (Proverbs 31:10–12 KJV).

According to God's pattern, no matter how much your husband may frustrate you at times, you must maintain an air of dignity and discretion. Keep the details of your family life private. Refrain from gossiping about him or depicting him in a negative light. In God's eyes, one of the worst things you can do is to humiliate or embarrass him: *"A virtuous woman is a crown to her husband: But she that maketh ashamed is as rottenness in his bones."* (Proverbs 12:4 KJV).

Praise Your Husband and Speak to Him Respectfully

Praise your husband as the Church praises Christ. Build him up—not just in front of others, but when you are alone together. Never speak down to him, as if he were a boy. Treating him like a child is demeaning and shows a tremendous lack of respect. You may not be aware that you are being condescending or disrespectful, but as a godly wife, you must take stock of your words and actions. Are you constantly criticizing or taking a parental tone with him? Remind yourself that you are his helpmate, not his parent.

Remember, you do not demand things of Christ. Rather, you make your requests known to him humbly, through prayer. Similarly, you must communicate your wishes respectfully to your husband, your spiritual leader, with the understanding that he deserves your respect as a man of God. Encourage his efforts to take the spiritual lead in your family. Demonstrating his value to you is essential to his well-being and development. It is also essential to the children who are watching the interaction of the Church toward Christ through their mother and father.

Remember, showing this level of admiration and respect for your husband will please God, who will bestow great blessings upon your marriage. What's more, it will draw your husband closer to you, as he will know he can always trust you. Most importantly, it will bring you closer to God, as you begin to show the character and integrity that He expects from you.

Guard Your Eyes and Heart from Temptation

Scripture contains many references to the importance of monogamy within the marriage covenant. In fact, the Bible teaches that sex outside marriage is a sin and a grave violation of God's law. God so despises adultery, Paul explains, that fornicators will not "*...inherit the kingdom of God*" (1 Corinthians 6:9–10 KJV). All that we are, all that we have—including our human desires—belongs to God. Even though sexual desire is a natural human trait, it must only be expressed within the marital bed. Our sexuality is a gift from God, and we must honour and express it within the boundaries He has set.

Throughout the New Testament, Paul refers to the Church as the body of Christ. Within this biblical metaphor, Christ has full authority over His body, the Church: "*And he is the head of the body, the church: who is the beginning, the firstborn from the dead; that in all things he might have the preeminence.*" (Colossians 1:18 KJV). This authority is absolute and ordained by God Himself: "*and hath put all things under his feet, and gave him to be the head over all things to the church, which is his body, the fulness of him that filleth all in all.*" (Ephesians 1:22–23 KJV).

Our bodies are part of Christ, and whatever we do to our bodies, we do to Christ. As a woman, you are also considered part of your husband's body. Remember what Adam proclaimed when he first saw Eve? "*And Adam said, This is now bone of my bones, and flesh of my flesh*!" (Genesis 2:23 KJV). He even chose to name her "woman," understanding that she was taken from the body of man.

You are part of your husband, and your body belongs to him in the same way that our bodies belong to God. If you are unfaithful, you will not only bring shame upon your husband physically, but spiritually, in essence bringing shame upon the Church and the body of Christ. You can see, then, why female chastity is precious to God. Your sexuality is a priceless gift that should be handled with care. Use it to express love for your husband and to produce children with him. Preserve yourself with the understanding that you are part of your husband's body.

Your body is a temple of the Holy Spirit and, as Paul reminds us, destroying that temple will incur God's anger. *"Know ye not that ye are the temple of God, and that the Spirit of God dwelleth in you? If any man defile the temple of God, him shall God destroy; for the temple of God is holy, which temple ye are."* (1 Corinthians 3:16–17 KJV). Just as members of the Church devote themselves to Christ, so must you devote your body to your husband. Giving yourself to another will cause great harm to your husband and invite God's wrath into your life.

In the Christ pattern, a woman's body belongs to her husband, and her husband is the head of her body. As such, he must care for her as he would his own body. This means he must do more than just devote his body to her. A husband must be prepared to lay down his life for his wife, as Christ gave his life for the Church: ""*Husbands, love your wives, even as Christ also loved the church, and gave himself for it;"* (Ephesians 5:25 KJV). Remember that your devotion to your husband will be reciprocated. If your husband is a man of God, he will love you sacrificially, as deeply and as profoundly as Christ loved his people, the Church.

For a godly wife, chastity is crucial, but she must remain faithful in all ways. That is, chastity is a virtue that requires faithfulness of body and mind. This means you must free yourself from all forms of infidelity, whether physical or emotional. ""*Flee fornication. Every sin that a man doeth is without the body; but he that committeth fornication sinneth against his own body."* (1 Corinthians 6:18 KJV). Not only must you practice conjugal fidelity, but you must also remain faithful to your husband in your words, thoughts, and deeds.

Respect yourself by living in pure and holy ways. Give your body to your husband alone. Lavish affection upon him and be generous in how you respond to his requests for physical intimacy. Set up boundaries and guardrails to protect yourself from temptation. For example, refrain from flirting with or fantasizing about other men. Treat your body as a temple of the Lord. Dress to show modesty and propriety rather than to draw inappropriate attention to yourself. By honouring your husband, you are honouring God. Obedience to the law of chastity will build trust and closeness with your husband. Likewise, obeying God's standard of sexual morality will serve to strengthen your connection to God.

Embrace Your Role as Keeper of Your Home

A godly wife is orderly and productive: "*She looketh well to the ways of her household, And eateth not the bread of idleness.*" (Proverbs 31:27 KJV). As keeper of her home, she works hard to care for her family and manage her home. In fact, Scripture compares her strength and resourcefulness to that of a merchant ship: "*She is like the merchants' ships; She bringeth her food from afar. She riseth also while it is yet night, And giveth meat to her household, And a portion to her maidens. She considereth a field, and buyeth it: With the fruit of her hands she planteth a vineyard. She girdeth her loins with strength, And strengtheneth her arms.*" (Proverbs 31:14–17 KJV).

She understands that God expects us to care for everything He's given us on earth, including our homes. Just as church leaders ensure the House of the Lord is kept clean and organized, a godly woman strives to create the most orderly environment she can for her family. Her feminine touch ensures her house is a peaceful, comfortable sanctuary to all who enter it.

Whenever you walk into a beautifully decorated home, you automatically assume it was designed with "a woman's touch." Most men have a hard time identifying what their wife does to make their home feel so welcoming and can't specify the small details that make a house a home. Husbands should be proud of their wife's efforts to beautify the home. ""*Through wisdom is an house builded; And by understanding it is established: And by knowledge shall the chambers be filled With all precious and pleasant riches.*" (Proverbs 24:3–4 KJV). Just as a church is made welcoming to all of God's children, so should your home be inviting to all who walk through its door.

There are many practical steps you, as a Christian wife, can take to begin to embrace your role as keeper of your home. Start by managing your home to the best of your abilities. Declutter and organize your house. Enhance your space while keeping your family budget in mind. Schedule your family's appointments, and work to build a stable, loving household, so you can free up time to worship as a family and study God's Word.

If these tasks begin to feel overwhelming, remember, being the keeper of your home doesn't mean taking on more than you can manage. God does not want you to feel stressed and unappreciated. Take steps to ensure this does not happen. Delegate to your children and husband where appropriate. Ensure that everyone is doing their part. When caring for your home, remember to take care of yourself as well. Your goal is not perfection, but a continuous journey toward a happy, healthy, God-focused home.

You can glorify God through your homemaking without becoming anxious and overwhelmed. Don't let an obsession with perfection deprive you of quality time with your husband and children. Setting realistic expectations for yourself will allow you to complete your tasks joyfully, as God desires. "*Whatsoever ye do, do it heartily, as to the Lord, and not unto men; knowing that of the Lord ye shall receive the reward of the inheritance: for ye serve the Lord Christ*" (Colossians 3:23–24 KJV). Understanding your value and carrying out your duties with enthusiasm and purpose will take you far in fulfilling your true God-given role in your family.

Grow Closer to God: Set Your Mind on Spiritual Things

A godly woman is spiritually minded. She understands that God greatly values this quality and expects it of all His followers. Paul reminds us in Romans 8:6 (KJV): *For to be carnally minded is death; but to be spiritually minded is life and peace.*" If you are a woman who desires a closer relationship with Christ, becoming holy-minded should be a top priority. But what, exactly, does it mean to be spiritually minded? Why should this be a goal in your marriage, and how does it bring you closer to God?

A spiritual woman is fiercely committed to her beliefs and refuses to be influenced by ungodly thoughts and actions. "*God is in the midst of her; she shall not be moved: God shall help her , and that right early.*" (Psalm 46:5 KJV). Being spiritually minded means placing yourself in the right mindset to model Christ (Proverbs 31:10–31). Christ is the cornerstone, and the Word of God is the foundation of all that we say and do (Acts 4:9–12; 1 Corinthians 3:9–15; 1 Peter 2:1–8). Adopting a spiritual mindset will strengthen your connection to Christ and help you to model Him in every aspect of your life.

While your husband is responsible for providing for your spiritual needs, you must also take it upon yourself to develop a closer relationship with Christ. In practical terms, this means looking at your life through a spiritual lens. It means allowing your spiritual beliefs to guide your everyday thoughts, decisions, and actions. It means keeping God's Word in your heart and mind and guarding against worldly mindsets and patterns.

God should be at the centre of all your actions, big and small. Demonstrate your devotion to Him by setting aside quiet time every day to read the Bible and reflect upon things of the spirit. Share your joys and challenges with Him. Draw nearer to him in spirit through prayer.

Remember that, through God, all things are possible. Open your heart to the opportunities revealed in His Word. Let Him show you how to keep your family on the right spiritual path: "*Trust in the Lord with all thine heart; And lean not unto thine own understanding. In all thy ways acknowledge Him, And He shall direct thy paths*" (Proverbs 3:5–6 KJV).

Consciously adopting a spiritual mindset will benefit your marriage in countless ways. You will influence your husband with your godly behaviour and help with his spiritual development (Romans 12:18–21; 1 Corinthians 7:13–17; 1 Peter 3:1–6). Motivated by your love of Christ, you will demonstrate a Christlike example for your kids. If you put your faith at the centre of your marital union, you will move closer to the Creator and seal your bond with Him.

Model the Church in Your Marriage Relationship

As we've learned, God's original design for marriage includes a clear order of authority in which husbands must love their wives and wives must submit to their husbands. Unfortunately, due to misguided modern interpretations, the concept of submission is often misunderstood. People today see it as chauvinistic or wildly out of step with the times. Even the word "submit" tends to make them feel uneasy.

When we look closely at Paul's teachings, however, we see that the biblical understanding of submission has nothing to do with modern perceptions. The apostle is not writing about a subservient wife being controlled by a domineering husband. Wives are not meant to be doormats, and husbands are not meant to be dictators. Instead, he is describing mutual submission (wives to husbands and husbands to wives). He is calling upon both husbands and wives to submit to God's wishes and willingly put God's desires above their own.

We know that in his writings, Paul demonstrates that marriage is rooted in the relationship between Christ and the Church. In fact, as we saw in chapter two, God designed the institution of marriage to hold the prophecy of Jesus and the Church. As such, He expects husbands and wives to mirror that relationship. Within God's pattern of marital leadership, both men and women have a unique role to play. A husband must love and treasure his wife as Christ loved and treasured the Church. He must love her sacrificially, to the extent he would give his life for hers. For her part, a wife must model the Church by submitting to her husband and showing reverence to his leadership role.

As a Christian wife, you are called upon by God to participate in this Christlike model of headship and submission. Paul writes: “”*Wives, submit yourselves unto your own husbands, as unto the Lord. For the husband is the head of the wife, even as Christ is the head of the church: and he is the saviour of the body. Therefore as the church is subject unto Christ, so let the wives be to their own husbands in every thing.*” (Ephesians 5:22–24 KJV). Your husband's role as spiritual head is ordained by God. By submitting to his spiritual leadership, you are modelling Christlike qualities in your marriage. Doing so will bring a new level of trust and joy to your union.

As you submit to your husband, remember, biblical submission is not about inequality. God did not create marriage based on dominance and inferiority. Strive to become a supportive partner to your husband. Read the Bible and pray together. Share your opinions, but let him make the final decision, trusting that he has your best interests at heart. Don't submit to him in a fearful or resentful way. Instead, show reverence to his leadership and focus on helping him fulfill his duties. Living your life as it was biblically ordained is a powerful way to embrace your role as a Christian wife and nurture your relationship with God.

WOMEN IN ABUSIVE MARRIAGES

When it comes to adultery and abandonment, the Bible is clear that divorce should be a last resort. But what happens when a woman is trapped in a violent or abusive relationship? How does God look upon divorce in this kind of extreme situation?

Through Scripture, we know that any sort of violence in marriage is considered an offence against God. In fact, the Bible condemns abuse of any kind. Under no circumstances should a woman remain in an unsafe situation or endure abuse or oppression of any kind.

While abuse, whether physical, mental, or sexual, is not grounds for divorce, a woman does not have to remain in a dangerous situation or tolerate her husband's violent behaviour. If you are suffering abuse, I encourage you to get out of danger as soon as possible. Call the police. Get to safety. Do what it takes to ensure your husband can no longer inflict harm upon you.

Remember, it's okay to separate while getting help to reconcile your marriage. Separating for safety's sake is a sensible and crucial first step. Only after you are out of harm's way should you begin to contemplate a way forward. In most cases, once your journey toward spiritual healing as a couple is complete, that path should involve reconciliation with your husband.

Pray for your husband. Seek out spiritual counselling together. Do the hard work it takes to heal your marriage wounds and fortify your bond. God intended marriage to be lifelong, and as a married couple, it is imperative that you exhaust every avenue to repair your marriage and build a loving, sacred union that reflects Christ's relationship with the Church.

If, however, the situation remains challenging and should your husband continue to be abusive or refuse help, it's imperative to lean on the guidance of God's Holy Spirit. This divine direction should be trusted above the turmoil of emotions or misleading thoughts. Let God's guidance illuminate your path and reveal the subsequent steps to take in such difficult times. The previous chapters revealed how, over time, men and women lost sight of God's true expectations for them within the marriage covenant. Influenced by a rise in worldly marriage patterns, couples no longer adhered to a biblical concept of marriage. Rather, they interpreted God's patterns in ways that suited their busy lives or obeyed His marriage laws selectively, ignoring those they found inconvenient. We learned that straying from God's original template had devastating and far-reaching repercussions for Christian marriages.

We saw, too, the remarkable spiritual and marital healing that occurs when couples begin to embrace God's original marriage patterns. To guide couples through this process, chapters three and four provided practical steps husbands and wives can take to apply God's original template. Some of these steps may not be easy to take and may require a degree of sacrifice on the part of the individuals in the marriage relationship.

As you begin to implement these strategies and adopt a spiritual mindset, you may start to question whether it's truly necessary to strictly obey God's instructions. You may see the value in following some patterns, for example, but question whether stringent adherence to all principles is necessary to glorify God. *Isn't it enough*, you may wonder, *to obey some of His principles if the overall intentions I have for my marriage are good*? *I'm doing my best in this*, you may think, *so why isn't that enough*?

In the next chapter, we'll explore answers to these questions. Biblical stories, I believe, tell us much about God's character and provide a clear indication of what He considers right and wrong. By considering the themes revealed in two of these biblical stories, we'll get a better sense of the weight of God's laws. Moreover, we'll begin to understand what happens when mankind obeys His heavenly patterns and what happens when we fail to follow His commands. God's marriage laws define and regulate how husbands and wives must interact with each other to honour and glorify God. And as with all spiritual laws and principles, there can be profound consequences for couples who fail to obey His marital commands.

FREQUENTLY ASKED QUESTIONS

What are some of the challenges faced by modern women in terms of balancing work and home life?

Modern women face numerous challenges in balancing their work and home life, including managing both their professional and domestic responsibilities. They often carry the mental load of keeping things running smoothly at home, such as childcare, caring for aging parents, and housework. This double burden can lead to stress, burnout, and negative impacts on their physical and mental well-being.

How does the modern interpretation of God's expectations for wives contribute to the challenges faced by women today?

The modern interpretation of God's expectations for wives has been distorted, leading women to lose sight of how to honour and fulfill their God-given duties within their marriage. This distortion adds to the pressure women face in trying to balance their roles as workers, mothers, and wives, contributing to their feelings of stress and being overwhelmed.

How can understanding God's true expectations for women help restore balance and purpose in their lives?

By understanding God's true expectations for them, women can learn to focus on the qualities that God expects them to demonstrate in order to live a righteous and fulfilling life. This understanding can also provide them with the knowledge and tools to fulfill their divinely ordained role, ultimately leading to a more balanced life that aligns with God's original marriage design.

What are some of the characteristics of a godly woman, and how can women apply them in their lives?

The Bible outlines several characteristics of a godly woman, and understanding these qualities can help women refocus their attention on God, fortify and protect their marriage, and become the true woman of God they are meant to be. By studying Scripture, women can uncover God's intended design for them and apply these qualities in their daily lives, leading to a more balanced and purposeful existence.

What are some qualities of a virtuous wife?

According to Proverbs 31, a virtuous wife is a God-fearing woman who maintains a deep connection to God throughout her life. She is generous and kind, and she always looks to the Lord for advice and comfort. Above all, she is completely devoted to her husband, loyal, and discreet, and she seeks every opportunity to raise him up in front of others.

How can a Christian wife embrace her role as the keeper of her home?

A Christian wife can embrace her role as the keeper of her home by managing her home to the best of her abilities. She can begin by decluttering and organizing her house. She can try to enhance and decorate her space while keeping her family budget in mind. She can schedule her family's appointments and work to build a stable, loving household, freeing up time to worship as a family and study God's Word. She should delegate tasks to her family members and prioritize self-care, setting realistic expectations for herself to complete tasks joyfully.

What is the importance of monogamy and chastity within a Christian marriage?

Monogamy and chastity are crucial within a Christian marriage because they honour the marriage covenant and adhere to God's law. The Bible teaches that sex outside marriage is a sin and a grave violation of God's law. By remaining faithful to one's spouse in body, words, thoughts, and deeds, a person honours their spouse and God. Obedience to the law of chastity builds trust and closeness within the marriage and strengthens the connection to God.

What does it mean to be spiritually minded, and why is it important for a godly woman?

Being spiritually minded means placing yourself in the right mindset to model Christ and allowing your spiritual beliefs to guide your everyday thoughts, decisions, and actions. A godly woman is spiritually minded because it strengthens her connection to Christ, helps her model Christlike behaviour, and is a quality that God greatly values.

How can adopting a spiritual mindset benefit a marriage?

Adopting a spiritual mindset benefits a marriage in countless ways. It allows a wife to influence her husband with her godly behaviour, which aids in his spiritual development. She can also demonstrate a Christlike example for her children. By putting faith at the centre of the marital union, a couple can move closer to the Creator and strengthen their bond with Him.

What is the biblical understanding of submission in a marriage, and how should a Christian wife participate in this model?

The biblical understanding of submission in marriage is about mutual submission between a husband and a wife, both submitting to God's wishes and putting His desires above their own. A Christian wife should participate in this Christlike model by submitting to her husband's spiritual leadership, not in a fearful or resentful way, but by showing reverence to his leadership role and focusing on helping him fulfill his duties. This will bring a new level of trust and joy to the union.

CHAPTER 5

Walking in Faith: The Consequences of Defying God's Laws

"O that thou hadst hearkened to my commandments! then had thy peace been as a river, and thy righteousness as the waves of the sea..." (Isaiah 48:18 KJV).

Through God's Word, we see there are specific patterns and principles He expects us follow to prove our love and demonstrate our faithfulness to Him. These divine laws set the standard for righteousness and regulate how we must behave in society. Most importantly, they reveal a great deal about God's character and heart. They demonstrate that while He is a loving and merciful God, He is also a holy God—powerful, omnipotent, and untouched by sin. As such, He must always be revered, respected, and obeyed.

Obedience, I believe, is an act of worship. It is also a powerful way to spread the gospel and ensure that future generations learn about God's holiness and power. The act of obedience carries with it great rewards. In fact, God's generosity toward those who obey Him is boundless. God promises that when we have faith and surrender to His Word, we will be transformed by the Holy Spirit and "*...filled with all the fulness of God*" (Ephesians 3:19 KJV).

As long as you walk in obedience and render service to God, you will receive the abundance of His spiritual blessings. Your well-being will be like a river, *"and thy righteousness as the waves of the sea"* (Isaiah 48:18 KJV). But what happens when you stray from God's principles? Does God expect you to follow His spiritual laws exactly, or can you compromise on those you deem less important or interpret them to better suit your personal needs?

The Bible offers countless examples of the significance of following God's commands fully, no matter how small or mundane. Through numerous biblical stories, we learn that applying God's commands incorrectly or for the wrong reasons can incur God's wrath and bring about tremendous grief and destruction. These stories reveal the principles behind God's rules and the consequences of failing to obey them. Let's examine two of these biblical teachings now.

OUT OF EGYPT AND INTO THE WILDERNESS: LESSONS FROM THE MOSAIC COVENANT

The Book of Exodus tells the story of the liberation of the Israelites from slavery, when God freed them from bondage and helped them escape their Egyptian oppressors. Through Moses, God led the Israelites out of captivity and into the wilderness, where He made a sacred covenant with them. This covenant, the Mosaic Covenant, contained God's promise that if the Israelites obeyed Him in all things, they would become His treasured people, a holy nation perpetually free from harm because they were forever under the protection of God.

God told Moses exactly what to tell the Israelites after they witnessed His immense power as He freed them from slavery. Tell them this, God said to Moses, *"ye have seen what I did unto the Egyptians, and how I bare you on eagles' wings, and brought you unto myself. Now therefore, if ye will obey my voice indeed, and keep my covenant, then ye shall be a peculiar treasure unto me above all people: for all the earth is mine: and ye shall be unto me a kingdom of priests, and an holy nation..."* (Exodus 19:4-6 KJV). With these words, God made clear that He intended to take the Israelites as His chosen people and make Israel into the greatest nation on earth.

But a covenant is a two-way agreement. In exchange for His loyalty and protection, God expected the Israelites to become a model nation, diligently representing His character and upholding His standards here on earth. In other words, God expected faithful adherence to His instructions in all aspects of their lives. And through Scripture, we see that God wanted them to demonstrate their loyalty and obedience to Him in detailed and specific ways.

For example, when God wanted the Israelites to construct a portable temple that would allow Him to dwell among His people, He instructed Moses: *"And let them make me a sanctuary; that I may dwell among them. According to all that I shew thee, after the pattern of the tabernacle, and the pattern of all the instruments thereof, even so shall ye make it."* (Exodus 25:8–9 KJV). God intended the Tabernacle to be an exact copy of the true temple in heaven, and to serve as a space of worship where priests could perform their daily sacraments, sacrifices, and offerings. Because of its sacred nature, God gave Moses explicit instructions on how the Tabernacle was to be built.

The Making of God's Tabernacle

Even before the Israelites began constructing the Tabernacle, God warned Moses: *"...Moses was admonished of God when he was about to make the tabernacle: for, See, saith he, that thou make all things according to the pattern shewed to thee in the mount."* (Hebrews 8:5 KJV). They were to use certain colours, for example, because they were symbolic. When the Israelites used blue, they were representing the heavenly nature of Christ. When they chose gold, they were representing the deity of Christ, and when they chose purple, they were representing the royalty of Christ. Red was symbolic of the blood of Christ. And when they used brass materials, they were symbolizing Christ's humanity.

In keeping with these patterns and symbols, the Tabernacle was divided into two separate compartments, The Holy Place and The Most Holy Place. In the first compartment stood a table of showbread, a golden candle stick, and an incense burner. The candlestick was symbolic of the illumination of the Holy Spirit. The incense burner symbolized the prayers of Christ for the saints, and the bread symbolized Christ, who is the bread of life.

Within these detailed patterns, God was teaching the Israelites about Jesus Christ, as Christ is the ultimate model for life. Everything about the construction of God's Tabernacle in the wilderness proved that God is a God of patterns. What's more, His patterns of worship and ways of living constantly pointed forward to the Way, the Truth, and the Light, which is Christ.

Divine Retribution: The Perils and Pitfalls of Disobeying God

So, we know that if the Israelites followed God's patterns correctly, He would bless them beyond their wildest dreams. *"Blessed shalt thou be in the city, and blessed shalt thou be in the field. Blessed shall be the fruit of thy body, and the fruit of thy ground, and the fruit of thy cattle, the increase of thy kine, and the flocks of thy sheep. Blessed shall be thy basket and thy store. Blessed shalt thou be when thou comest in, and blessed shalt thou be when thou goest out."* (Deuteronomy 28:3–6 KJV). If they deviated from God's patterns, however, they would be afflicted and cursed.

The Israelites turned out to be fickle servants, often forgetting about or intentionally defying God's instructions. And each time they did this, God's response was swift. Whenever they fulfilled His patterns correctly, they were rewarded in abundance. Nations submitted to them and there was peace throughout the land. But when they misinterpreted His patterns or violated them for the sake of a selfish agenda, the Israelites felt the wrath of a vengeful God.

Zephaniah notes that when the Israelites forgot God's goodness and began to walk by sight, rather than faith, when they acted with hypocrisy or turned from God to worship false idols, God said, "*...Surely thou wilt fear me, thou wilt receive instruction...*" (Zephaniah 3:7 KJV). And when they forgot to fear Him, God promised "*...to gather the nations, that I may* *assemble the kingdoms, to pour upon them mine indignation, even all my fierce anger: for all the earth shall be devoured...*" (Zephaniah 3:8 KJV)

Through Zephaniah's description of God's interaction with the Israelites, we get a glimpse of both the depths of God's mercy and the devastating force of his wrath. Through this biblical story, we learn that God cares deeply about how we demonstrate His patterns. This applies as much in our marriages as in our daily lives. God's marriage pattern must be followed correctly because they, too, point back to a greater truth. We must demonstrate Christ in how we live our married lives. In fact, the more we apply God's marriage patterns and obey His marriage laws, the better we model the love between Christ and the Church.

Uzzah and the Ark of the Covenant

There is another story, the story of Uzzah, which demonstrates the importance of walking in faith and obeying God's instructions, principles, and commands. Housed within the Tabernacle was the Ark of the Covenant, the most sacred vessel of the Israelites. This large, gold-plated wooden box was adorned with two magnificent golden angels that faced each other and were connected at the wing tips.

In addition to a pot of manna and the rod of Aaron, the Ark held the tablets of God's law, which God had given to Moses at the top of Mount Sinai. These symbols of faith were extremely significant to the Israelites, most notably because it was within the Ark of the Covenant that God's presence could dwell. The Ark was revered by the Israelites because it represented the physical manifestation of God's presence with them.

After being captured by the Philistines, the Ark was eventually returned to the Israelites. Wanting to bring it safely back to Jerusalem, King David had a new ox cart built on which to transport the Ark. During the journey, they came upon a smooth area of land called a threshing floor. It was there that one of the oxen stumbled, and the Ark trembled and shook.

Instinctively, Uzzah reached out to stabilize it, immediately incurring God's wrath. God's response was swift, and the result was tragic: "*And the anger of the LORD was kindled against Uzza, and he smote him, because he put his hand to the ark: and there he died before God.*" (1 Chronicles 13:10 KJV). But why did God react this way? Why would He take the life of a man who meant well and was simply trying to prevent the Ark from falling to the ground? When we take a closer look at Scripture, we begin to better understand the reason for God's fury.

Defiance Leads to Sin and Death

Just as God had provided detailed instructions on how to construct His Tabernacle in Exodus 25-27; Numbers 4:5-15, we see that He also described the way the Ark of the Covenant was to be moved. When transporting the Ark, the Israelites had been commanded to place wooden poles through its rings and to hoist it on the shoulders of the Levite priests. In choosing to transport the Ark on an ox cart, David was directly disobeying God's command.

What's more, God had specified that only the Levites, the priests who were responsible for defending His honour, were allowed to touch the Ark while it was being transported. Numbers 1:51 (KJV) states: "*And when the tabernacle setteth forward, the Levites shall take it down: and when the tabernacle is to be pitched, the Levites shall set it up: and the stranger that cometh nigh shall be put to death.*"

At first, David was angered and confused by the severity of God's reaction. Why would God strike this man down in the prime of his life when he was only doing his best to protect the Ark? What David eventually came to realize was that in taking Uzzah's life, God was sending a clear message to His people. He was letting them know how imperative it was that they honour His wishes and obey His commands.

We know that, as a holy vessel, the Ark deserved to be treated with great reverence and care. This clearly did not happen. First, by ignoring God's instructions on how to transport and handle the Ark, David was delivering a brazen insult to God. Second, by reaching for the Ark rather than shouting out a warning, Uzzah was presuming that God needed him to catch it.

Implicit in Uzzah's action was the assumption that he was more powerful than God, a sin that was punishable by death.

Had God allowed Uzzah to catch the Ark and live, He would have sent the wrong message to the spiritual realm. Allowing Uzzah to successfully catch the Ark would have symbolized that humanity had the ability to save God from falling. This idea is blasphemous and incorrect, as we know that human beings simply do not possess that kind of power. God does not need saving. It is always we, His people, who need to be delivered from the darkness, and it is through the power of the Almighty that we will be delivered from our sins.

In the end, we see that although Uzzah had good intentions when he tried to steady the Ark, his good intentions were not enough to spare him. God's power is unsurpassed. He is a great and powerful God, and it is always His people who need Him and never the other way around. God is also a righteous God, who protects His heavenly patterns through His laws. Despite his good intentions, Uzzah had to die for his defiance of God's spiritual laws.

Applying God's Spiritual Principles to Your Marriage

From the story of Uzzah, we learn that despite being well-intentioned, Uzzah's failure to learn and live by God's spiritual principles had unintended, tragic consequences. Had Uzzah understood God's principles regarding the Ark, he would have realized that because the Ark was under divine protection, there was no need to try to save it. Instead of reaching for it, he would have stood back and shouted out a warning that the Ark was about to fall.

We know that when God decides to protect something, there is nothing that can stand in His way. As Scripture says, when you put your faith in God, He will instruct His angels to protect you: *"For he shall give his angels charge over thee, To keep thee in all thy ways. They shall bear thee up in their hands, Lest thou dash thy foot against a stone."*

(Psalms 91:11–12 KJV). In other words, had Uzzah refrained from intervening, God's angels would have swooped down from heaven and caught the Ark before it ever hit the ground.

When it comes to our lives, we must pay close attention to these biblical lessons. We must recognize that God takes very seriously the correct demonstration of His heavenly patterns. Moreover, we must learn to apply His spiritual patterns completely, faithfully—without questioning or amending them. We must learn that the cost of disobedience can be severe.

With respect to marriage, this lesson is especially critical. God sees marriage as the most important human bond because it is a sacred union that reflects His image. Unfortunately, folks today marry and divorce without any regard for God. They do so without grasping the implications of breaking a covenant with God, one that was designed to demonstrate the future coming of Christ and the birthing of His Church.

It is your responsibility to be obedient to God in your marriage. This means submitting to Him wholeheartedly and making every effort to understand and apply His spiritual principles in your married life. As we've learned in this chapter, obedience is pleasing to God and will bring about great blessings in your marriage. Defiance, on the other hand, is abhorrent to God, and your marriage will suffer consequences when you fail to obey.

If you are experiencing difficulties within your marriage, you may need to examine your understanding of and adherence to God's marital laws. Are you following His marriage principles completely or, like David and Uzzah, are you ignoring or acting in defiance of God's laws? Remember, you may have the best of intentions regarding your marriage, but none of that matters if you are violating God's spiritual laws. No matter how well-intentioned you are, failing to obey Him or straying from His marriage template will invite His anger.

As a Christian, you must recognize that to glorify God within your marriage, you must follow His commands exactly as He instructed. You must place Him at the centre of your marriage and apply His marriage principles without question or amendment. The Bible is brimming with stories that teach the importance of obedience and the consequences of defiance. These narratives demonstrate one common theme—that disobeying God's laws and principles will provoke His anger and good intentions will not be enough to spare you from His wrath.

FREQUENTLY ASKED QUESTIONS

What is the significance of obedience in the context of faith and worship?

Obedience is an act of worship and a powerful way to spread the gospel, ensuring that future generations learn about God's holiness and power. It is also the means through which believers receive the abundance of God's spiritual blessings.

What does the Bible teach about the consequences of failing to obey God's commands?

The Bible offers numerous examples that show the significance of following God's commands fully, no matter how small or mundane they seem. Failing to obey God's commands can incur His wrath, bringing about tremendous grief and destruction.

What was the Mosaic Covenant and its significance for the Israelites?

The Mosaic Covenant was a sacred covenant made between God and the Israelites, in which God promised that if the Israelites obeyed Him in all things, they would become His treasured people, a holy nation perpetually free from harm under His protection.

What can we learn from the construction of the Tabernacle?

The construction of the Tabernacle teaches us that God is a God of patterns, and that His patterns for worship and ways of living constantly point back to Christ, who is the ultimate model for life.

What were the consequences for the Israelites when they deviated from God's patterns?

When the Israelites deviated from God's patterns, they were afflicted and cursed, and they felt the wrath of a vengeful God. However, when they fulfilled His patterns correctly, they were rewarded in abundance, and there was peace throughout the land.

What lesson can be learned from the story of Uzzah and the Ark of the Covenant?

The story of Uzzah demonstrates the importance of walking in faith and obeying God's instructions, principles, and commands. Despite having good intentions, Uzzah's failure to adhere to God's spiritual principles led to tragic consequences.

How does God view marriage?

God sees marriage as the most important human bond because it is a sacred union that reflects His image. It is a covenant designed to demonstrate the future coming of Christ and the birthing of His Church.

What is the role of obedience in a successful marriage?

In a successful marriage, both partners must be obedient to God, submitting to Him wholeheartedly and making every effort to understand and apply His spiritual principles in their married life.

How can disobedience to God's principles affect a marriage?

Disobedience to God's principles can bring about negative consequences in a marriage, as disobedience is abhorrent to God. To receive His blessings and protection, couples must strive to follow His commands and principles in their marriage.

How can believers ensure they are following God's principles in their marriage?

Believers can ensure they are following God's principles in their marriage by studying Scripture, praying for guidance, and seeking wise counsel from others who understand and follow God's marital laws. This will help them to understand and apply His spiritual principles in their married life, leading to a strong and blessed union.

CONCLUSION

Marriage is the building block of human society. It was designed by God, for His purpose, at the time of creation. Through Scripture, God provides the laws and principles we must follow to live our marriages according to His truth. Contained in God's Word is His original template that, when applied correctly, will let you grow in faith as a couple. Adhering to His template honours God and helps you fulfill your spiritual calling. It's never too late to incorporate these principles into your marriage! Regardless of the state of your union, demonstrating His patterns will let you walk together on God's path to a righteous marriage.

This book laid out God's original marriage principles, as found in Scripture. In chapter one, we learned that the turmoil and confusion in contemporary marriages is due to the influence of worldly values. Because of false, modern interpretations of God's original design, men and women have retreated from their God-given roles and neglected to obey His patterns correctly. In fact, there's a great deal of confusion about God's true expectations for married couples. As couples get caught up by the pressures of daily life, they lack the tools to apply His original patterns and fall short in achieving their true purpose, oneness with God.

Further into the chapter, we observed that a dramatic shift in marriage roles occurred at the start of World War I, as women entered the workforce to replace men who'd been called away to fight. For the first time in history, men were no longer the primary providers for their families, and women no longer devoted most of their time to managing their homes.

The general expectation was that, once the war was over, women would return to the home and men would reclaim their role as provider. By the end of the World War II, however, it was clear that women were in the workplace to stay.

No longer relied upon as breadwinners, men's confidence and self-worth began to suffer. Without a sense of purpose, husbands were set adrift, desperate to find a place in this unfamiliar, new family structure. Some became resentful and lashed out at their wives. Others became despondent or gave up on their marriages altogether. Men had forgotten that God's true purpose for them had nothing to do with their ability to serve as financial providers.

For wives, the joy and personal fulfillment they expected from greater economic freedom simply did not materialize. Without the support they needed, having to split their time in a million directions resulted in high levels of stress and burnout. Like men, women had lost sight of their true purpose, as ordained by God. Women were overlooking the fact that God's expectations for them had nothing to do with their ability to juggle life's many tasks. Husbands and wives needed to be reintroduced to God's original patterns and reminded of God's true expectations for them within a marriage covenant. And they needed to learn to model Christ in their marriages, so they could begin to glorify and honour God.

Chapter two took a closer look at God's original design for marriage, including His spiritual patterns and how they should be applied in marriage. Here, we learned that when you enter a marriage covenant, you make are making a sacred agreement with God to abide by His spiritual principles. We saw that God's original design contained the prophecy of Christ and the Church and that God expects us to model this relationship in our relationships.

God is a God of patterns, and every marriage pattern ensures the marriage covenant will forever represent our relationship with Him. Every pattern is constant and eternal, and every pattern, when obeyed, will result in a peaceful and stable family environment. Likewise, every pattern, when disobeyed, will displease God, and bring about discontent in your marriage.

Modelling Christ within our marriage is one of God's most important expectations of us. For husbands, this responsibility is especially significant. As the God-ordained head of the household and spiritual leader of his family, God holds the husband responsible for the spiritual well-being of his wife and children. However, as we've seen, many men don't know how to demonstrate their pattern correctly in contemporary marriages.

To help men demonstrate the correct pattern, chapter three provided useful ways a husband can restore his position of leadership in the home. If you're a man struggling with inadequacy and displacement in your marriage, I encourage you to revisit the strategies I've provided. Remind yourself that God's expectations of you aren't confined to your skills as a financial provider. As spiritual head, God has called upon you to provide in other important ways.

Support your wife however you can, be it physically, financially, or spiritually. This includes providing the physical security and emotional support she needs throughout her day. Protect your wife. Love her sacrificially. Be willing to give your life for her, as Christ gave his life for the Church. Present her blameless and refrain from speaking negatively about her to others. Initiate prayer with her, read the Bible together, and take the reins as her spiritual guide.

While all these components of God's marital pattern are vital, when showing your devotion to her, always go above and beyond. Sometimes, the smallest acts of support make all the difference. For example, when my wife and I walk together, I always make a point to open the door for her. I do this to lighten her burden, and I do this because I would like God to open doors for me. Speak softly to her. Share your heart with her, and be aware of her needs. By modelling Christ in every interaction with her, you'll better demonstrate the relationship of Christ and the Church.

In chapter four, I offered practical ways a woman can fulfill her higher calling to support her husband in his position of spiritual leadership. As we saw, there are many ways you, as a godly woman, can do this. Be virtuous and discreet, never bringing shame upon your husband. Embrace your role as keeper of your home. Speak to your husband with kindness and respect. Save yourself for him alone. Giving your body to someone else will destroy your husband spiritually and bring about the judgment of God.

Take responsibility for your own spiritual development, but always be a loving and willing follower of your husband's spiritual lead. Remember, you are a precious jewel to him, and he will always have your best interests at heart. Encourage his leadership efforts, and be generous with your affection for him. Seek out his knowledge and guidance as you strive to grow closer to God. Go above and beyond whenever the opportunity arises.

Of course, there are instances when a woman may feel her husband is not making godly decisions. If she is strongly opposed to the choices he is making, it may become difficult to submit to his lead. She may want, desperately, to follow biblical principles but be conflicted by the fact that she deeply disagrees with the choices her husband is making for their family.

To prevent this occurring in the first place, I always remind those couples I have the opportunity to counsel pre-maritally of the importance of choosing the right partner before entering into a marriage covenant. When illustrating this point, there's a beautiful story I like to share about the mating rituals of the American Bald Eagle.

When choosing her mate, the female eagle will carry a branch high into the air and then drop it directly in front of the male she's considering. She does this to test the suitability of her potential mate. If the male returns her interest, he will swoop down, collect the branch, and return it safely to her. By returning the branch, the male is demonstrating his suitability as a match and proving his ability to fulfill her needs.

We can all learn something, I believe, from the intricate courtship rituals of these beautiful animals. Just as the female eagle carefully watches and assesses a potential mate before bonding with him, so must we ensure the person we're considering as a life partner is a match for us physically, emotionally, and spiritually. In other words, we must purposefully put stops and checks in place *before* we move forward into marriage.

Unfortunately, many women leap into marriage, propelled by the butterflies of love, and when the dust eventually settles, they realize they've failed to do their due diligence and are now yoked to a mate whose values are different from their own. They find themselves questioning his decisions and are at odds with having to follow his spiritual lead.

If you, as a Christian woman, find yourself in this situation, I encourage you to talk to your husband honestly about your areas of concern. Communication is everything. If your husband is a decent man, he will take what you're saying into consideration. If your husband genuinely understands that you are his helpmate, he will carefully consider and evaluate your concerns.

In all of this, seek God's wisdom. If there are certain areas where you make better decisions than your husband, perhaps he will see the wisdom in having you make the decisions in those cases. For the most part, however, you should be able to trust your husband's judgment and respect his God-given role as spiritual leader of your home.

Chapter five highlighted the importance of following God's laws completely and the sometimes-tragic consequences of failing to do so. Through the story of the Israelites, we saw a people discovering the pattern of Christ in the wilderness and beginning to learn the consequences of disobedience to God.

Through God's instructions for the building of His Tabernacle, we learned that God is a God of patterns. Whenever the Israelites deviated from these patterns, they were overcome by nations, impoverished, or captured and scattered to the wind. We saw, too, that when they followed His patterns, they grew closer to God. As a reward for their obedience, they became righteous among nations, were exalted by God, and blessed beyond their wildest dreams.

We also considered the story of Uzzah, the young Israelite who lost his life trying to prevent the Ark of the Covenant from falling to the ground. When King David made the decision to return the Ark to Jerusalem on a cart rather than hoisted on the shoulders of priests, as God had commanded, he was directly violating God's law.

When the cart tipped and Uzzah tried to steady it, God responded by striking him down. Naturally, King David was horrified. He couldn't comprehend why God would react so severely to someone who was only trying to protect the Ark. In trying to steady the holy vessel, wasn't Uzzah just responding as anyone of us would have? Surely Uzzah was well-intentioned, as his first and only instinct was to safeguard the Ark of God.

While, on the surface, it seemed as if Uzzah lost his life merely for trying to protect the Ark; in reality, he had to die because God was sending a message. What David later came to realize, and what we all now know, is that good intentions are simply not enough. In this case, it was Uzzah's good intentions that led to sin and the defiance of God's laws.

Had God allowed Uzzah to catch what He deemed a physical representation of the presence of God—had he had been permitted to catch the Ark and live—the message He would send back to the spiritual realm was that mankind was capable of catching God. This notion is blasphemous and untrue! Mankind does not possess that kind of power, and it is a mortal sin to presume that we do. Uzzah's well-intended actions were not enough to save him.

They say the road to hell is paved with good intentions. This is just as true in our marriages as it is in our daily lives. Once we enter the marriage covenant, we must trust God's marriage laws implicitly. We must adhere to them precisely as God instructed or suffer the consequences of His wrath. We often like to live our married lives with good intentions, but as we've seen, good intentions are not enough. God is very specific about His pattern and how He expects us to demonstrate of our knowledge of Christ in the way we live our lives.

As I mentioned in the beginning of this book, there is nothing you can't accomplish as a married couple once you become aware of, and learn to apply, God's pattern for marriage correctly. It is my sincere hope that the information presented here will assist you in this endeavour.

As you work through your marriage conflicts to fortify your relationship, I encourage you to look back at these chapters as often as you need to. And as you assess your progress, ask yourself if you're truly following God's pattern or reinterpreting them for your own convenience. Always remind yourself of the consequences of deviating from His original plan.

See yourself through God's eyes. Are you doing all you can to strengthen your bond with your spouse and help your marriage thrive? Remember, marriage is a beautiful picture of the gospel, created by God to reflect Christ's love for His people, the Church. As a couple, you must work in union to demonstrate this Christ-Church model every day of your married life.

To fortify your marriage, live to glorify God in your everyday life. Everything you do as a couple should be aimed at serving God. Nothing you do should diminish His beauty and His glory. "*Whether therefore ye eat, or drink, or whatsoever ye do, do all to the glory of God.*" (1 Corinthians 10:31 KJV). All that you are—every thought, prayer, and action—should model the life of Christ and reflect your love of God above all things.

Dear God,

As we come to the end of this journey of learning about marriage through "Marriage God's Way," I pray that the words written in this book will not just be words on a page but seeds that grow and flourish in the hearts and minds of those who read it.

I pray that the teachings and principles shared in this book will take root in the readers lives and transform their marriages into reflections of Your love and grace.

May they remember to always seek Your will and guidance in their relationship with their spouse, and may their love and respect for one another continue to grow each day.

Thank You for granting me the strength, dedication, and persistence to write this book. I pray that the hopes and expectations for its impact will be realized in the lives of those whose lives it touches.

I ask all of these things in the name of Jesus Christ, our Lord and Saviour.

Amen.

About the Author

Daniel Wynter has been a certified Christian marriage counsellor for over a decade, steering couples toward harmony, understanding, and love.

He has been happily married for many years to his beloved wife, Nadeen. They have a daughter and a granddaughter, giving him first-hand experience with the joys and challenges of family life and making his counselling realistic, practical, and compassionate.

An accomplished scholar, Daniel has a degree in theology, and he is pursuing his master's degree.

Daniel is the lead pastor and Bible study teacher at Open Arms Church of Jesus Christ in Pickering, Ontario, Canada.

In his leisure time, he finds solace in nature, including long walks and quiet moments by the lake. Daniel is also an avid reader and writer, always eager to explore new ideas and deepen his understanding of the world.

Find out more about the author at www.danielwynter.com

Printed in the USA
CPSIA information can be obtained
at www.ICGtesting.com
CBHW020829040824
12617CB00035B/430